on loan to Library

YOU CAN ALWAYS BEGIN AGAIN

*Also by Ladislaus Boros
and published by Search Press*

THE MOMENT OF TRUTH
PAIN AND PROVIDENCE
WE ARE FUTURE
GOD IS WITH US
IN TIME OF TEMPTATION
LIVING IN HOPE
MEETING GOD IN MAN
HIDDEN GOD
MEDITATIONS
OPEN SPIRIT
PRAYER

YOU CAN ALWAYS
BEGIN AGAIN

LADISLAUS BOROS

Translated by David Smith

PAULIST PRESS
New York/Ramsey/Toronto

This book is published for the first time in English translation in 1975 by Search Press Limited 2-10 Jerdan Place, London SW6 5PT Great Britain

Published originally in German under the title *Gedanken über das Christliche* by Josef Knecht, Frankfurt am Main, Federal Republic of Germany ©Verlag Joseph Knecht 1973

U.S. Edition, © 1977 Search Press Limited, Printed under the title: *You Can Always Begin Again.*

Library of Congress
Catalog Card Number: 76-49324

ISBN: 0-8091-2006-2

Published by Paulist Press
Editorial Office: 1865 Broadway, N.Y., N.Y. 10023
Business Office: 545 Island Road, Ramsey, N.J. 07446

Printed and bound in the
United States of America

Contents

Contents

Foreword

This book was originally published as a series of articles in a journal. I think that the editor's introductory words are still relevant:

'Man loses himself if he loses the centre of his being. He will never have time if he doesn't take time in order to have time. The Christian will never know what it is to be a Christian if he thinks of his Christianity simply as being active. Many people are coming to realise this nowadays. But what can they do to find the centre of their being, to have time and to live as Christians from that centre?

'Man—if he is to be really man—is in search of an answer. I have asked a theologian who has already helped many people to go ahead—"on the way"—to write a series of articles on what a Christian should think about in prayer and contemplation. In these meditations he applies his usual sensitivity to a Christian's inner life.'

The editor has hit on the main point here. At the same time, I must ask the reader to take everything that I say not as a final statement, but as a stimulus to further thought. I hope that what he reads here will lead him to go on looking for truth—the truth that is God.

Ladislaus Boros

The kingdom of God

The kingdom of God

Jesus came to reveal God, the God who has sovereign power in the world. He came to tell us what God thinks of us, what he wants of us and how we stand with him. He came to proclaim what God intends to do for us. He came to announce redemption and grace and to disclose the new creation. What part do we play in this? If we are to become Christians, we have to accept God's activity in Christ at the deepest level of our being—whatever the consequences may be. We must do that whether it deepens our experience or not, and whether we live more harmoniously and perfectly because of it or become more fragmented and disrupted.

How can I make that clearer? The best way is to consider the biblical idea of the 'kingdom' which was the content of all Jesus' thought, preaching and activity, and even the substance of his life, death and resurrection.

Two of his sayings come to mind at once and show us which direction we should take. In Mark 1:14, he says: 'The time is fulfilled and the kingdom of God is at hand'; and in Luke 17:20–21: 'The kingdom of God is not coming with signs to be observed; nor will they say, "Lo, here it is!" or "There!" for behold, the kingdom of God is in the midst of you'.

It would have been easy enough for Jesus to transform the world by magic. Instead he chose to be insignificant, to give himself totally and to bring about an inner kingdom of the heart in that way. That is the essence of a true Christian's inner life. Jesus himself became every man's brother. He gave hope to every man and was a friend to the oppressed. He accepted all the limitations of being human with all the strength of his humanity and his divinity. He fully embraced the risk of being a man.

The man Jesus lived as it were from within. He did not lead a double life, a life of pretence, constantly deceiving others. On the contrary, his life was straightforward and without cunning. He was there for others: for the suffering, the oppressed and the underprivileged; for those without power and status in the world. During his public ministry, he never worked miracles to satisfy a whim, to achieve his own ends, or to make himself popular. His aim was above all to establish an inner dynamism in the world, a power which would function in secret, a principle of life in each of us which would inwardly form and transform the world.

Jesus didn't come to solve the problems that man himself can and should solve. He came so that all men should have a friend in him: a brother who makes peace, brings about reconciliation, and speaks well of everybody.

What is particularly striking in his preaching is his insistence that all those who wanted to follow him should hate no one and never repay evil with evil. In fact he went further and called on them to love their enemies. He wanted above all to give hope to all men. Therefore he defended the sinners against those who were called just, and protected children and those who were defenceless. He had a simple respect for every creature and was deeply sensitive to life as such. His whole way of life was simple and unobtrusive. He chose to forgo power not because he was weak, but because he wanted to be near to all men. There can be no kingdom of God without this quality of not hating.

In the second place, Jesus took pleasure in quite every-day things: in a good meal and a refreshing drink, in a simple walk with his friends. He always avoided dazzling his fellow men with appearances. Even his suffering wasn't ostentatious: he cried out, sweated blood, and felt drained and forsaken. He always gave men hope. To the broken man beside him on the cross he said: 'Today you will be with me in paradise' (Luke 23:43). He had a youthful spirit and was completely unafraid of the princi-palities and powers of this world, even the inner powers which lived in men. His life was marked above all by utter freshness and an inspired ability to change. His whole existence was one single message of joy—the 'good news' in person: 'These things I have spoken to you, that my joy may be in you, and that your joy may be complete' (John 15:11). The fruits of his Spirit are 'joy, peace, patience and kindness' (Gal. 5:22). Because man is able to live so close to Jesus he is also able to 'rejoice with unutterable and exalted joy' (1 Pet. 1:8). There can be no kingdom of God where there is ostentation and where there is no joy, peace, patience or kindness.

In the third place, Jesus tried above all to be nameless. He was lonely in the way that the depths, the mountain peaks and the oceans are lonely. If we really want to pene-trate to the heart of the mystery of Christ, we too must learn how to be quite alone for long periods. Only then will we be able to grasp what is essential in Jesus' existence, because it was from his loneliness that his Word came. He was alone as he grew up. He was alone when he was tempted in the wilderness. He had to depend on himself alone in all the decisive moments of his life. Without any selfish intention in mind, he contemplated the things of this world and thus came to understand their essential nature and at the same time how to include the world in his own experience. He expressed himself in a totally earthly way, and the allegorical language of the parables flowed through his veins like blood. His calm and balanced attitude emerges clearly from his objective and economical way of speaking, which at the same time always pointed towards the Absolute. There can be no kingdom of God where famous names and important personalities abound.

In the fourth place, Jesus was silent. He listened. He was not pushing, but receptive, and so he was able to break the power of habit and overcome the effects of dulness in his life. He created within himself a space where encounter with others could really take place. His receptiveness to others was so great that those who met him as a friend called him simply a 'good man'. This is not perhaps the most profound or significant of christological statements; and yet anyone who has experienced real goodness in his life—possibly in times of bitterness or suffering—will know that only a God-man is really capable of making it completely true. There can be no kingdom of God where there is no human goodness.

In the fifth and last place, Jesus came from a family that was poor in every sense of the word. What is more, he made no attempt to correct this situation. His own poverty was first of all of a reluctance to make claims for himself. Everything that he did resulted in apparent failure. Again and again his words, his actions and sufferings were misunderstood. Reading the gospels carefully, one is again and again struck by Christ's isolation as a bitter experience which did not, however, embitter him, and by his silence despite all that he said: 'The darkness has not understood the light' (John 1:5). He fully accepted his own inexorable fate. He himself wasn't understood or recognized; but he accepted that and carried it patiently with him to his death. His non-acceptance by others reached an absolute limit when he died forsaken by God. There can be no kingdom where men make insistent claims for themselves.

The kingdom of God, then, isn't something permanently fixed and established. It is something living which comes towards us. For a long time it was very remote from men, but it came closer and is now so very near to us that it longs to be accepted by us. The kingdom of God is simply God ruling within us.

God knows everything yet says nothing

God knows everything yet says nothing

In the depths of his being, modern man no longer feels that God is with him in all the events of his life. He has no sense of going through life as it were hand in hand with his creator. He is no longer conscious of God's nearness to him. Precisely how and why that has come about I can't go into here. I can only affirm that in recent years man has undoubtedly entered a sphere of existence in which he no longer experiences God directly and in which God is apparently no longer with him in all the decisive moments of his life. Therefore he has to break almost violently out of his ordinary sphere of existence if he is to come close to God.

Prayer is extremely difficult today because God has undeniably become less communicative. He is more silent. In saying this, I am simply confirming what most people today know from their own experience. Of course it would be foolish to think that God does not intervene in the confusion that prevails in the world, since that is certainly not his way of acting.

What we all know today and often find depressing is that God sees everything, hears everything and knows everything, yet says nothing. So many quiet, unobtrusive Christians who give so much of themselves in their lives long to hear his voice speaking a word of recognition and encouragement—yet he says nothing. How many broken or utterly lonely people there are who call to him in their suffering, yet he gives no sign of his closeness to them and says nothing. We could give many more examples, but one stands out above all the rest.

It is the example of Christ himself, confronted by his enemies. They accused him, condemned him and mocked him—yet God said nothing. On the cross, Jesus prayed, crying out with a loud voice: 'My God, my God, why hast thou forsaken me?' God still said nothing.

God's silence is not new, but it seems to depress us now more than it did men in the past. This is probably because we experience it in a more extreme form and because we are obliged to come to terms with it. In our powerlessness and anxiety, we ask again and again: is there any purpose in talking and praying to a God who says nothing?

We are afraid that God is really absent. We are pained by his silence, which is beyond our understanding. We always knew it, of course, even though we may never have taken it seriously enough, but, because of that fear and that pain, we come to feel—however vaguely—the transcendence of God. We begin to sense that he is exalted far above everything that exists or can be thought of outside him.

We cannot as yet hazard an answer to this question of God's silence to our prayer. It is something that will only become clear to us very gradually. But we can say without hesitation that, despite the sometimes depressing silence of God, a Christian is bound to go on depending on prayer. He may do endless good. He may relieve distress and suffering again and again. He may be completely open to the Church and the world and give himself totally to others. But if he is not open to God, something essential is lacking.

We are all in one way or another restricted. None of us is completely free and completely flexible in God's hands. That is why we are all bound to implore him: Lord, don't pass by until I have become aware of your coming! Lord, don't stop knocking at my door, hammering and pushing until I have opened it to you! The man who is ready to open to the Lord is above all always quiet. His whole being is one single Yes to God. The Christian who achieves most and who is most inspiring is the one who is quiet and who has learned to listen to God.

We penetrate to the heart of Christian life not when we speak, but when we say nothing. That happens only when we are quite recollected and open the door of the inner room of our Christian experience to allow God's presence to make itself felt. We have to learn to be quiet. We have to resist the constant noise and chatter in the world. The external hubbub is, however, only one part of the danger and perhaps not even the most serious one to overcome. It is more difficult to deal with the inner danger—the turmoil of our thoughts, the ceaseless urging of our desires, the restless movement of our spirit and the blank wall of our apathy.

Our inner life often seems like a spring blocked by stones. If we are to live properly, we have to learn how to remain silent. We can begin by simply holding our tongue whenever we have to show respect for another person or carry out our professional duties and inspire confidence. This is, however, no more than a beginning and an attitude that should be almost automatic in a Christian. We must do more and develop the habit of saying nothing when we want to speak and even when we feel we ought to speak. We should try to overcome all tendency to be voluble and to talk without reflecting. How many unnecessary things each of us says in the course of a single day. And how many silly things. We have to learn that silence is good in itself and that it is not an empty void, but an expression of a full and authentic life.

But even that is not enough. We have to go even further. From learning how to be externally silent, we must learn the value of inner quiet. We must acquire the habit of dwelling peacefully and quietly on a serious question, an important task or the memory of a person for whom we are concerned. If we do that, we shall eventually come to experience the deep, inner world more and more, until ultimately we reach the point of quietness in the presence of God. All excitement, bustle and noise break down in the face of the one who transcends all that we can ever think or feel.

Jesus' public life lasted at the most three years and many people think it lasted barely two. What a short time. And how important were the thirty years that went before, the time in which he did not teach or preach, engage in public debate or work miracles—the silent years. There is surely nothing more attractive in the whole of Jesus' life than his silence, and we ought always to be alert to the sound of this silence and, in deep reverence, to be in tune with it as an expression of his inmost being. He preferred silence to speech, purity to success and the boundless generosity of love to achievement. To Jesus the inner life was all important.

Was that because he was by nature idle? Not at all. We know that a great deal of the short time during which he was active was taken up with this inner life. Only fragments of some of the events that took place during those few years are reported in the gospels, but we know that those events were important, because we are told that he prayed and made decisions 'in a lonely place', or 'in the hills' (Mark 1 : 35; 4 : 46). He prayed before choosing the Twelve and, before his trial and death, in the garden. All that he did externally was built on a foundation of prayer.

This points clearly to a principle in the life of faith of every Christian. We must remember this whenever the struggle is raging most fiercely, words are being spoken most loudly and work is engaging us most consciously. We must remember at such times that everything that is loud and insistent will eventually become silent. Everything that can be seen and heard will be brought to judgment. All that is wrong now will be put right. The unspoken will be revealed as strength. What is concealed will prove to be decisive and what is not based on inner quiet will pass away. Only what derives its strength from within will be able to enter the new and eternal creation.

How was this reflected in Jesus' attitude during his trial? He neither defended himself nor attacked anyone. Above all he did not look for help from anyone. He even said, at the decisive moment, what his opponents needed to hear in order to destroy him. He did not try to prevent his own destruction. But his silence was not a sign of weakness or despair. It showed that he was present, recollected and ready.

You can always begin again

You can always begin again

Providence is surely one of the most important terms in the Christian vocabulary. But nowadays it is no longer a word which prompts an echo in the mind of every Christian who hears it—one which has only to be spoken for everyone to understand it in all its shades of meaning. The Bible contains many such words and throughout the history of the Church they have constantly come to the surface, enjoyed a meaningful existence for a time, pointed the way to revelation and faith, and then perhaps sunk into oblivion again for a long time. Today we have brotherly love, future, hope and many others, but we can look in vain in our list of present-day key-terms for the word 'providence'.

That is regrettable, since it is undoubtedly a concept which can provide us with a vital insight into the nature and ultimate being of man as a creature who prays, and into the essential goodness of God. There can be no time in the whole history of man's salvation which could benefit more than our own from a real understanding of the meaning of God's providence.

Modern man is almost instinctively opposed to injustice. Yet injustice is a form of providence expressed within a magical view of the world. Attempts are made by magic to compel God to use his power in the service of man. According to the Christian view, on the other hand, man should submit to God's power. A modern man's objections to this view of providence are usually very clear. A few people discover the trick of dealing with life's problems and then work everything their way. If providence were, however, simply a placing of God at the service of man in everyday affairs, then it would be no more than an expression of a selfish human impulse and therefore pure magic.

God himself has in any case condemned this magical interpretation of his providence. That is clear from the Book of Job. A statement such as 'You are a better person if everything is going well with you' has no place at all in the Christian understanding of man and the world, because the very opposite is often closer to the truth. There are, after all, so many people who are totally orientated towards God, but whose lives are quite unsuccessful. They seem to encounter every misfortune and always to be in a place where the lightning strikes. The Christian conclusion, then, is that the message of providence is a divine wisdom and consequently a proclamation of joy and liberation to God's friends: that is, to those who are afraid or depressed. What this providence means in the last resort is: If there is no one left to help you, if you can see no way out of your difficulty, think of God who is always with you and will always stand up for you.

We must ask seriously whether this message of providence is not the same as what Paul called 'hoping against hope', when he said of Abraham that 'in hope he believed against hope' (Rom. 4:18). Those who suffer misfortune are in a special sense God's favourites precisely because, without God, they would have no hope at all.

God's providence can be described as a change of mind,

an inner transformation. It does not mean that God will miraculously intervene in our lives and remove all danger of attack. On the contrary, it means that there is no ultimate way out of our difficulties. Everything could stay as it was before. The danger may not disappear from our lives. We may have to go on living with our fear and depression. God's providence means, however, that, despite all this, everything has in fact changed. In and through all our suffering, God's goodness has appeared. We can therefore say: This thing is hurtful, but basically it doesn't really count.

Of course, in the Bible and the Old Testament especially, there is a current near to the surface which would seem to disprove this view of God's providence. Israel is often told that it will be successful and that victory will be achieved over its enemies. That, however, is on the surface—there is a deeper current running through the history of the people: an expectation of consolation in disaster, a hope of final release from oppression.

That undercurrent is expressed most clearly in the prophetic and the Wisdom books: 'Fear not, for I have redeemed you; I have called you by name, you are mine!' (Is. 43:1) 'You are precious in my eyes and honoured and I love you' (Is. 43:4); 'Even though I walk through the valley of the shadow of death . . . thou art with me' (Ps. 23:4). 'The Lord is my light and my salvation; whom shall I fear? The Lord is the stronghold of my life; of whom shall I be afraid?' (Ps. 27:1); 'He who listens to me will dwell secure and will be at ease, without dread of evil' (Prov. 1:33); 'If you sit down, you will not be afraid; when you lie down, your sleep will be sweet. Do not be afraid of sudden panic' (Prov. 3:24–25). There are countless examples of Israel's confident expectation of salvation.

God's promises of eventual salvation led to the growth in Israel of a new dimension in the people's understanding of faith. They developed an attitude of trust despite distress. It was of the utmost importance for their interpretation of providence that God should put them severely to the test and not allow them to be spared the blows of fortune. He wanted them to learn how to remain calm in extreme hardship and distress. It was as if he were saying to them: Your ultimate, inner being, the most important aspect of all, can never be taken away from you. It is in my mercy for ever. Even if everything collapses, my promise—heaven—will always be open to you.

The joy of being made inwardly free and the happiness of total trust in God despite everything is powerfully reflected in the New Testament and especially in Paul's message of hope in God's love: 'Who shall separate us from the love of Christ? Shall tribulation, or distress, or persecution, or famine, or nakedness, or peril, or the sword? . . . I am sure that neither death, nor life, nor angels, nor principalities, nor things present, nor things to come, nor powers, nor height, nor depth, nor anything else in all creation will be able to separate us from the love of God in Christ Jesus our Lord' (Rom. 8.35 : 38–39). This text expresses the Christian doctrine of providence concisely yet vividly. In Paul's own experience, nothing— no power in the world, no external danger, no human sin or fault and no psychological confusion—can in the long run overcome the power of God's grace.

Against all the passing evidence of this world and even against our own heart when it accuses us and makes us troubled and depressed, as Christians we should be able to let a supreme confidence break through. We shall in the end be saved. We should 'reassure our hearts before God whenever our hearts condemn us, for God is greater than our hearts' (1 John 3:19-20). Paul penetrates even more deeply into the mystery of God's providence in his letter to the Romans: 'In everything God works for good with those who love him' (Rom. 8:28). Paul doesn't qualify or restrict this statement in any way. Augustine, in his commentary, merely adds (logically): '—even sins'.

What has happened to us in the past, what we are now and what may take place in our lives in the future—all this is in a sense without significance. God's faithfulness and mercy are above everything, even sin and guilt. Everything in our lives can be given a new meaning. Everything can be a step on the way towards God. In Jesus Christ, God's mercy appeared among us and from him came the ultimate promise: 'Behold, I have set before you an open door, which no one is able to shut' (Rev. 3:8).

In Christ, God has made a new beginning possible for us. This possibility of a new beginning is always open to us in all the situations in which we may find ourselves. For God, no man is for ever lost. That is the essence and the inner promise of our faith in God's providence.

The new generation

The new generation

When God is being discussed, we are personally involved and have to begin to pray. A theologian—if he is really practising his art—doesn't deal with the 'problem' of God in the sense of trying to overcome it. On the contrary, he allows the mystery of God to overcome him. All true theologians have always lived in an atmosphere of prayer in which they have reflected about God. *Adoro te devote, latens Deitas*—'Godhead here in hiding, whom I do adore'. This was never pure poetry for a mediaeval theologian, but the basic principle of all theological thinking and knowledge—adoration of the hidden God.

Over many years spent in association with my fellow men and in study of their inner lives, a fairly clear portrait of the new generation has formed in my mind.

Soberness

Modern man is more critical, less trusting and more sceptical than those of the previous generation. He is more single-minded and more purposefully directed to his goals. His attitude is almost always determined by the work that he is called on to do. Although it changes according to his task, it is fundamentally listening to the truth of things: a devout attentiveness to the things of this earth. Modern men are conscious of idle talk, imprecision, differences of opinion, conflict and manipulation in society.

Men notice these faults not only in the arts, philosophy and religion, but in the leadership of Church and State. They know the qualities that are really needed if a true society is to be built up: soberness, clarity, attention to what is essential, objectivity without illusions, and self-discipline.

Self-surrender

The new society must be quite free of all that marks the present establishment. It must be free of all arbitrary elements. Its members must overcome all desire to exert power over others or to manipulate them. The new, free society that has to be built up must be totally unlike the existing constraint. The basic laws of the life of the community must be derived from the objective nature of things. That calls for self-surrender on the part of those building up the community. The ultimate criterion is what exists independently of the subject: what is objectively true.

This attitude makes enormous demands. Man has to learn to deny himself and to give himself entirely to others. He has to learn no longer simply to carry out orders in subjection to those in authority. The old social attitude has to give way to a new 'objectivity'. In the new order of society towards which men are striving, there can be no people who simply carry out orders in unquestioning obedience; there can be none who simply give orders.

All men must be guided by an inner sense of discipline and obedience to the objective essence of things. If a task to be done with others is very complicated, then those taking part in the communal enterprise have to join in close working groups. Total commitment to the objective truth and to each other, and mutual agreement and tolerance, are fundamental aspects of this task of forming the new community.

Silence

For these people, the whole world, including its inhabitants, is one great field of experimentation, the raw material from which a new world and a new society has to be fashioned. There is no part of the world that is forbidden territory. At present man is applying his power to change society to his fellow men; in the course of this task his own being is, as it were, diminishing. He is listening more and more to the hidden magnitude of the work to which he has dedicated himself. The result is that he speaks less and less about himself, and, when he does so, is very reticent. But his silence is an expression of concentrated strength.

What does this mean? A new kind of recollectedness has resulted from man's accumulated psychological experience. This attitude is basically a stability and peace born of a deep conviction that the world is ultimately good. We can be certain that we are following the right course, men now feel, so long as our attempts to shape the world accord with its fundamental laws. What has to be combatted is any attitude which obscures our vision and makes men assert themselves rather than affirm that the world is good and holy. This affirmation of the world is ultimately an echo of the fundamental revelation at the beginning of the Bible: 'And God saw everything that he had made, and behold, it was very good.'

Friendship

I have drawn attention to certain aspects of the attitude of modern man. These all point to his extreme objectivity and would seem to indicate that intersubjective relationships such as love and friendship are impossible or at least very difficult for him. In fact, the very opposite is true. Precisely because he approaches the problems of life today with such cool objectivity, he is all the more alert to the differences between human beings, and to the uniqueness of an individual. He does not reduce personal encounters with others to the level of self-interest, but accepts them as pure gifts: as something that is given to him and which he can give. We encounter modern man most fully in his most profound insights in thought and faith at the intersubjective and personal level.

Honesty

A young Christian today sees himself especially as someone who is seeking. Since the Second Vatican Council he has found the courage to talk openly about faith, to venture into new territory and radically to overhaul the traditional way of approaching and understanding faith. This new courage is in no sense prompted by a desire for novelty. It is the product of a spirit that has at last been awakened. It is marked by a fundamental honesty: by an openness to all truth, whatever its origin, and by a determined search for what is right. At the same time, a modern Christian's view of God has been radically purified.

Possessing a more authentic faith, we have been freed from the temptation to attribute to human values and systems what belongs exclusively to the Absolute. Faith is no longer triumphant, nor is it pure propaganda. It is now increasingly effective in personal witness.

Faith today

Faith today

Men today are seized by something quite new and powerful.

Towards the world

I suspect—although suspicions of this kind cannot be proved, they can be quite accurately sensed from the general mood and inner disposition of mankind—that an entirely new kind of saint is emerging in the Christian world today. He is a person who wants above all to testify to the truth of the order of God's creation and to listen attentively to the moment of grace; to remain flexible, open and clearsighted. He is always ready to carry out his Christian task wherever and whenever the need arises. In any situation, he will act on the historical imperative and give himself fully and unsparingly on the basis of the 'glory' of the Christian principle. He is always aware that if he is constantly ready to serve, but is never emphatic or direct in imposing his Christian faith, he will enable grace all the more fully to enter into the world in which he lives and works.

In these new saints, the world—and that also means the whole of society and human history, including above all the future—is once again transformed, sometimes painfully and usually unostentatiously, into God's own possession. A quiet and non-violent change takes place: an inner revolution, a transformation of the heart.

The phrase 'a change towards a Christianity of decision' has recently been applied to the younger generation of Christians, and it is certainly true that young people are nowadays looking more and more for personal and charismatic elements in their own lives. In bearing witness to Christ, they are not satisfied simply to keep to the more important elements in Christianity, to confess the truths of faith, and to fulfil the principal moral teachings of the Gospel or the Church.

On the contrary, a young Christian knows that he must make a personal choice and bear witness to the presence of Christ in his own life—a presence that is always the same, yet always different. By his own decision, his life has to be made into an expression of the mind of Christ. He knows very well what this search for God in the deepest ground of his being means. For many centuries it has been known by the hackneyed phrase 'the imitation of Christ'. This following of Christ is not an anxious, dispirited jogging along behind the Master—keeping up with him as best as one can. It is rather bearing individual witness in grace and charismatically to the mind of Christ in every situation in which one finds oneself and sometimes even in situations in which Jesus himself was never placed.

In bearing this kind of charismatic witness the dimension of Christ himself is revealed in all its depth in the life of the believer. In this way, a Christian can, in his own life here on earth, 'complete what is lacking in Christ's afflictions' (Col. 1:24). If we grasp this, we shall understand why young people are so powerfully seized by the person of Jesus today. In Jesus, a young man or woman is aware of everything that is good, authentic, original and sincere in his or her own life. Young people often complain of the way in which priests and ministers have made it difficult for them to penetrate to the depths of the mystery of Christ and in which they have simply answered their questions about Christ with clichés.

Demand

I often meet young Christians today who examine their reasons for choosing a particular career with enormous care. These young men and women do not allow themselves to be driven into a new situation in life simply by some unreflecting impulse or even because of such acceptable reasons as favourable working conditions, high financial rewards or good prospects.

On the contrary, they ask themselves seriously whether they will really be able to serve God in their chosen career. The basic question that they ask is: Shall I be able to 'save my soul'? Shall I be able to live in such a way that I shan't be forced to be insincere. Shall I be able to express my love for my fellow men?

This kind of thinking about the reasons for choosing a career in particular and about ultimate reasons generally (for they belong together) is a clear sign of vitality in a Christian. The future, after all, belongs to a person who makes demands and marks off his future aims in the 'not yet'—in what can't be humanly attained. A faith that makes such a decision possible can't be inherited like a family heirloom. It can't be found in the cradle or a baptismal font. It can only be acquired as a gift by giving oneself entirely. In this act of self-giving, the Christian makes God visible in the world. He becomes the incarnate wonder of the encounter with Christ.

Christianity is not a religion of external miracles. The wonder of Christianity is taking place at the level of Christian existence itself. The Christian himself is a wonder—a sign of God's presence in the world for other people. The believer himself is full of spiritual power, grace for others. The more he tries to be that grace, the more he and others will find it. That may be the essence of the new spirituality that is emerging in Christianity today—that we encounter God in our fellow men. A modern believer is inclined—and the emphasis that he places on this teaching may often be one-sided—to place Christ's talk about the last things (Matt. 25 : 31–46) at the heart of his understanding of faith and to regard it as the only valid criterion for every theological statement.

Clericalism in retreat

In the Church today, we are witnessing the disappearance of clericalism, not only in its external form, but as an attitude of mind. This process is of the utmost importance for the future of the Church.

External clericalism is in retreat. That means that the Church is rapidly losing the excessive influence that it has for so long exerted in many countries on the political life of the state and in society as a whole. What is happening, in other words, is that religion is no longer being misused for political ends.

The other form of clericalism is, of course, an 'inner' clericalism. That too is disappearing. Lay people are far less exposed to being treated as immature and dependent by a paternalistic clergy. Both forms of clericalism are based ultimately on a desire for power and that is something which Christ emphatically rejected. The more fully the Church tries to change, not just externally, but above all inwardly, the more successfully it will do God's work, and the more decisively it will fulfil its supernatural mission.

Questions people ask

Questions people ask

Whenever people begin to talk about the most profound questions of Christian life and faith today, not academically, but in an atmosphere of prayer and meditation, the conversation always takes a serious turn. That isn't surprising, since such questions are, after all, concerned with man at the deepest level of his existence. And they are very difficult to put into words. We ask them hesitantly and with great uncertainty.

For me, listening to them has always led to serious reflection. Over the years I have picked out a number of recurrent themes in the questions asked by believers. They recur because the most recent questions have always been the oldest ones: those that are fundamental to Christian life at all times.

The absence of God

For a modern man, the God-question included a need to reflect theologically about the nature of atheism and unbelief. A clear and yet subtly-shaded theology of atheism and unbelief is a prerequisite for anyone who wants to talk seriously with young people. When they ask questions about God, they are often asking whether it is possible to experience God authentically in the modern world—a world in which God doesn't really seem present. In any attempt to give a theological answer to this basic question, we must take a modern man's painful experience of the absence of God seriously, and indeed share in that experience ourselves. In faith, we have to try to show others how they can really discover and experience God at this particular time in history.

The Christ-question

This is a universal question. It is asked within the framework of a history of salvation in which all men are included and have always found themselves. In my experience, young people especially are quite capable of being moved by a deeply christological vision. This vision is based above all, on the one hand, on the letters that Paul wrote during his captivity to the Ephesians, the Philippians and the Colossians and, on the other, on the history of salvation and revelation in a world in which Christ is seen as the climax of man's development (Teilhard de Chardin is an especially inspiring teacher in this respect, so long as care is taken to avoid the continuous undertones in his writings which impress many young people today as mythological).

Redemption is universal

That anyone should be excluded from the salvation brought by Christ, that redemption should not be universal, is something that young people especially just can't accept today. This is one of their most insistent questions; they often ask it with profound unease. Again and again, they object to the tag 'Outside the Church there is no salvation', and variations on it.

I have never ceased to be surprised by the scandal that this statement causes, because I have never found it to be purely negative or destructive. Quite the opposite. One has only to apply one of the simplest rules of logic to the statement, 'There is no salvation outside the Church', and to express it in the reverse form, to obtain a different version with an entirely liberating effect : 'Wherever there is salvation, there is the Church'. This can be reduced to the simplest basic formula : *ubi ecclesia, ibi salus = ubi salus, ibi ecclesia.*

Understood in that sense, this controversial doctrine is a positive assertion of freedom. What was scandalous becomes liberating. The Church is always present—in its effects and in what may be a concealed form—wherever people are sincerely trying to do what is good, fine and true; giving themselves totally to what is greater than themselves; serving their fellow men with utter dedication; and wholly committing themselves to a cause. Everywhere where this is happening, salvation is taking place. Everywhere where this is happening, the Church is.

The question of man
Nowadays all people are looking for a (theological) answer which will reveal man as experienced in an existence which means more than the animal and at the same time rational being of abstract metaphysical thought. There is a great need for a Christian understanding of man which will emphasize the original unity of nature and grace, and not banish what Christians call 'grace' to a sphere outside and beyond man's concrete existence. We urgently need a Christian theory of man which takes fully into account such things as friendship, love, virtue and the experience of absurdity and death, and doesn't simply hand them over to moral theologians or the writers of pious books.

Confession and prayer

Among all these difficult problems about Christian life and faith, one still crops up again and again: 'I can't confess or pray any longer'.

Rightly or wrongly, Christians nowadays are unable to accept the attitude which used to be called appearing before the Almighty with a clean slate. How do we answer the question? We can point out that confession is there above all for us to free our friends, the people we love, from the poisonous effects of our sinfulness.

Human life is essentially life with other people. If I carry sins around with me, they are bound to enter the whole community with which I am so closely associated. If, on the other hand, I am sorry for my sins and confess them openly to a representative of the church community to which I belong, then I can free my friends in the community from the burden of my misery.

Why should we go to confession? So that we can be reconciled with God and thereby help to make the whole world, our closest friends and the very state of being man cleaner. So many Christians who go regularly to confession think only of themselves. That is a frightening fact. Confession is often a purely selfish act. When it isn't a service to others, it is not really confession at all and brings no increase of salvation into the world.

Finally there is the problem: 'I can't pray any longer'. In avoiding prayer, modern man isn't running away from God, but from himself and his superficiality. He doesn't want to escape from the infinite holiness of God, but from the barren emptiness of his own soul. We can make it clear to men in flight from themselves that simply waiting for God in silent readiness *is* prayer. Indeed, it is the most profound form of prayer that man in his torn and suffering state can offer to God. Suffering in itself, an inner experience without prayer, is simply prayer. The most urgent task confronting the theologian today may well be to elaborate a theology of prayerful life for modern man at the present stage of the history of salvation.

Theology today

Theology today

What expectations do people have nowadays of a theologian who will take the risk of talking about the mysteries of faith? In the first place, they expect him to prepare what he is going to say with care and to wrestle with the concepts and images that he uses. They won't accept fragmentary thoughts thrown out at random or thoughtlessly scribbled key-words. They want every statement that a theologian makes to be well thought-out, and every idea that he suggests to be well supported.

I know theologians who work for more than forty hours on a single talk or sermon that takes less than an hour to give. But their thought is so complete and yet so simple, and is expressed in such carefully-chosen yet straightforward language, that their listeners are seldom aware of any lengthy preparation. Something luminous emerges in the course of such meditations: clear thinking, a deep respect for the mysteries of faith, sound piety and, ultimately, truly poetic expression.

People also hope that the person who speaks to them about God will do so sincerely, truthfully and dynamically. I have often thought about the ideal of the 'meditative' theologian and would like to suggest some of the characteristics which, I believe, such theologians possess or should possess.

These theologians undoubtedly take the concrete situation in which they and their fellow men are placed as their point of departure. They introduce into theology a note of great longing and dissatisfaction with life as it is. They are 'progressive' in the best sense. They are critical and therefore know that, in the confusion of our world, what at first sight seems fine, certain and meaningful could be the outward appearance of evil.

They are spiritually calm and sober. Their vision is incorruptible. They are truthful and sincere in their approach to the mystery of faith. At the same time they are strangely uncertain, yet their very hesitation makes them attractive. They avoid easy solutions and obvious explanations. Their theological thinking is constantly accompanied by prayer and a personal association with God. They oppose prejudices and preconceived ideas and regard nothing as impossible until they have tried to do it. They don't venerate the triumphalism of theological manuals and respected theologians. They are always reluctant to divide the world into opponents and allies. On the other hand, they regard stupidity as one of the greatest sins, since their greatest happiness is in clear, realistic thought. Above all, they think charismatically and they are deeply concerned to address others with all their cares, their responsibilities and even their despair. They can give no answer to questions asked by their fellow men, and they don't hesitate to admit that.

These theologians are also convinced that any theology which does not in some way or another lift up man's spirit, praise God and lead to more friendship and love in the world isn't, in the last resort, theology. And so they try to do good to their friends in what they say and write. One result is that a discerning listener or reader can detect a note of serious responsibility in everything they say. They are aware that their ideas are a judgment on themselves, and that their own salvation depends on what they tell others. What they are trying to find in their 'professional' thinking is, quite simply, grace for our times.

They have a deep sensitivity and a fundamental openness to what is new or has not yet been recognized. They hope to change the world by new thinking. They think of theology as moving forward from initial ideas in an effort to make life finer and more translucent and to help their friends to overcome periods of discouragement and failure. For them, theological reflection is a humble service to man's life in order to protect and preserve everything that is worth protecting and preserving.

Their point of departure is their own experience of the suffering and distress of man's existence in the world. They don't struggle to achieve success or status. They are aversive to all forms of facile apologetics, but respond quickly to sharp debate and always stand up for the truth. They never try to score victories over others just for the sake of winning.

They never forget that only those who have experienced the depths of human misery, only those who have suffered on the cross, can speak words of freedom. Their thinking emerges from their having been put to the test. It occurs where goodness and friendship exist, and where men wait humbly and patiently until the truth they serve grows and bears fruit.

There are two other basic attitudes characteristic of a contemporary theologian. The first is an attitude of dissatisfaction. Whoever thinks that he can see must watch that he doesn't fall. That is a biblical warning. God seems to say to us: 'Don't be satisfied with your life as it is. Try to be more: to go beyond what you have already attained. You have to bear witness to the fact that human life is always moving towards new happiness. As soon as you begin to think that everything and everybody ought to be as you are now, you're not really a Christian any longer'. In giving this warning, God has put a holy dissatisfaction in the hearts of all Christians, and especially in the hearts of Christian theologians. The theologian of the future-present is called upon to think authentically as a Christian with the future constantly in mind. If he doesn't do that, his very being will become stunted and sterile. He must never regard his theology as closed.

The second basic attitude is defined by revelation as 'bringing forth fruit with patience' (Luke 8:15). God, the sower, wants us to be good soil. 'As for that in the good soil, they are those who, hearing the word, hold it fast in an honest and good heart, and bring forth fruit with patience.' That is a very accurate description of the theologian's life. We theologians have received the grace to be living at a time when the old ways of thinking are breaking down and a new world is being proclaimed. That new world of great promise does not come to us simply as a matter of course. It rises up from within our whole being. If we don't bring this new way of thinking about ourselves, it won't happen, and the old cart of the Church will go on rattling around in the future as it has in the past.

If we really want to renew the Church, we must first undergo a radical change of heart ourselves. We must accept this good and promising grace in our good, changed hearts; store and preserve it there; hold it fast and, in an act of total commitment involving the whole of our being, bring forth fruit. This we must bring forth with a determination and a toughness that can simply be called patience.

Both these theological attitudes have been summarized strikingly by Isaiah: 'Remember not the former things, nor consider the things of old. Behold, I am doing a new thing; now it springs forth, do you not perceive it? I will make a way in the wilderness and rivers in the desert' (Is. 43 : 18–19).

Friendly to all creatures

Friendly to all creatures

In becoming man, God accepted the whole human reality. He accepted everything that is ordinary, tiring, repetitive and inconspicuous and made it his own. This warm closeness of the Redeemer to man is very firmly expressed in the New Testament by the first three evangelists. Matthew, Mark and Luke wrote what are called the synoptic gospels because they present the reality of the Lord synoptically: that is, from the same viewpoint.

These gospels together form a remarkable document and the Christian should come to have a warm relationship with the three synoptic evangelists. They say nothing at all about most of Jesus' life; and the events which they do describe are written down in a very loose order, grouped according to individual preferences and narrated with many individual differences. All three evangelists, however, are interested in certain special events in Christ's life. They write anecdotes. This gives the synoptics their life and warmth.

They all draw attention to the physical presence of Jesus the man. We feel better after reading the synoptic gospels because they enable us to experience the enormous human attraction of the Redeemer. We grasp something of the great power that he had over the hearts of men. Reading the synoptics, we can understand why Peter and Andrew left everything at a word from Jesus and why the sons of Zebedee followed him without a moment's hesitation. It was the same power that made the people of Israel follow God into the desert and far from care and protection. The human heart finds its real home in Christ.

In the synoptic gospels, we meet a Lord who ate, drank and slept like all other men. He helped sick people and blessed children, but he also got tired and had to rest like all of us. He rejoiced in the nearness of God and his heart was full of the Father's will. He felt such sympathy with his fellow men that at least once it caused him to weep. People followed him because they knew that he pitied them in their neglected state. He invited all who were labouring and heavy laden to come to him. He showed tenderness to every living being. He taught the truth in a luminous and vivid way, but without euphemisms or sentimentality.

He did not value outward appearances. He did not plan his life carefully in advance, but lived by what was unexpected and surprising. He could wait for a long time until a human being was able to open his heart to him. He could also be insignificant, ordinary, average and poor. His friends were ordinary people. He respected the situation in which his fellow countrymen found themselves. He patiently accepted the political authority in the land and obeyed the religious institutions of his own people. At the same time, he was in no way tied to, or restricted by, all this and was conscious of his inner freedom. The way in which he accepted things as they were and did not try to change them by an externally revolutionary process is almost frightening.

At the same time, however, he made what was quite

unusual shine out in this very ordinary life. His whole being was luminous with holiness. God ruled in him and made his great power and authority more gentle so that it was gracious, mild and good. Something quite uncanny was present in this man—friendliness towards every creature.

The synoptic gospels bring us into contact with a man who did not break the bruised reed or quench the smouldering wick. This man could say: Come to me and you will find rest for your souls. He was deeply aware of our distress—the distress of the widow of Nain, of the poor sick women who only dared to touch the fringe of his garment and of the apostle who betrayed him. With one glance he could bring this apostle to repentance and forgive him. He was a man who had nothing at all to hide and could therefore speak the truth to everyone. He could stand before all men in a luminous simplicity of heart and move their hearts.

One of the highest aspirations of Christian contemplation is to experience the friendliness of the Lord. The believer is always attempting to come closer to the events in Jesus' life and thus to make him present in his own life and imitate him in all things. With patience, he penetrates more and more deeply into Jesus' reasons for acting and speaking as he did. He tries to relate his own words and deeds to Jesus's and, as he does so more perfectly his own inner life becomes more complete and he is filled with joy and a sense of belonging. Then the reality of Christ himself begins to shine through a Christian's life.

A Christian's purpose is to allow the inner law of Jesus' life to take visible effect in his own situation. The more this happens—the more fully a Christian says Yes to life—the more he helps the oppressed and the more he befriends the anxious. Jesus is God's grace given to us, a grace which made his face shine as if transfigured. Grace means graciousness, beauty and loveliness. These qualities flow into the world through the life of a Christian.

A Christian has the task of showing the world that the only person who can effectively reveal the deep, inner power of love is one who lives close to Jesus. Christ, the incarnate Word, is the place of creation, the place where truth and goodness appear in the radiance of glory and become beautiful. This means that a Christian, in his imitation of Christ, must offer the world the most beautiful, moving and impressive image that it is possible to present in creation. By concentrating the life of Christ within himself, a Christian can create a luminous space filled with God in our secular society. In a Christian there is a power that cannot be measured: the power of the presence of Jesus himself in the world. This is the real meaning of the much used and even hackneyed term the 'imitation of Christ'. Following Jesus is not anxiously trotting after him trying to keep in step. It is much more than this. It is letting the goodness and friendliness of the Lord shine through us in all the different situations in which we find ourselves, even in situations in which Jesus himself perhaps never was.

A Christian has therefore above all to bear witness in his life to the life of Jesus. He can't be satisfied with clinging to what is most important in the teaching of the Church, a mere confession of the truths of faith, or just carrying out the moral demands made by Jesus. His task is to live the life of Christ luminously for his fellow men.

He has to concentrate the presence of Jesus within his own inner being. That presence said Yes to life, had pity on all creatures, and was absolute goodness and simple friendliness to all men.

John's prayer

John's prayer

I have already spoken of Christ's friendliness towards all men and our reaction to it. This, however, is only a first step towards a much greater and deeper experience of Christ. We become more powerfully shaken as, in our study of the gospels, we penetrate more deeply into the mystery of the revelation of Jesus. It seems quite impossible to find a purely human explanation for Christ's pure humanity, for his simple and utterly selfless goodness and for his complete openness to man's distress and suffering.

The man Jesus is marked by great warmth and human closeness to others. Precisely in this the remoteness, the total otherness, of God breaks through—that aspect which cannot be explained in purely human terms. Again and again we are overcome by that holy awe of which John speaks in the Book of Revelation: 'Then I turned to see the voice that was speaking to me, and on turning I saw seven golden lampstands, and in the midst of the lamp-stands one like a son of man . . . His head and his hair were white as white wool, white as snow; his eyes were like a flame of fire, his feet were like burnished bronze, refined as in a furnace, and his voice was like the sound of many waters; in his right hand he held seven stars, from his mouth issued a sharp two-edged sword, and his face was like the sun shining in full strength. When I saw him, I fell at his feet as though dead' (Rev. 1:12–17).

In this vision, Christ is presented as greater than life.

His whole being is seen as luminous and radiant. Behind him is an abyss full of light and stars. He himself is full of the Spirit, powerful and creative. He is like the wind and the sound of many waters. All being is concentrated in him and the whole world, made one, also becomes luminous in him. On his face shine the lights of the universe.

The entire gospel of John is also full of this experience of Christ. Clement of Alexandria called it the 'spiritual' gospel because the concrete existence of Christ is made translucent by John and points throughout the whole of his gospel to the eternal mystery of the Logos, the second person of the Trinity. In the fourth gospel, all outward appearances are removed and the eternal being of Christ is laid bare. The unfathomable inner depths of the God-man become visible in John.

Before anything had been created, Christ was already present, since eternity, with God, because he himself is God. Everything that was created came about through him. The whole universe bears his features and, by bearing his features, is. He is the element of life in all life, the element of light in all light and the splendour of all creation. Unbelievably, this eternal being of light, this splendour of God's eternal glory, entered the world of darkness. Like a flash of lightning, he passed through our dark universe, enlightened it briefly but powerfully and returned to the unknown sphere of his glory.

When God illuminated the world with his Son, a light was suddenly thrown on all things; a powerful light shone into the hearts of all men. All that was confused, base and evil in the world became visible. The light of Christ was God's judgment of man.

That judgment was, however, at the same time redemption. In shedding his light into men's hearts, God made it possible for them to come to a decision and those who decided for Christ had to undergo an inner revolution. Anyone who opts for Christ has to allow his whole being to be changed, since it is only in that way that the world can ever become quite full of the light of the Lamb. The new heaven and the new earth really come into being when this decision is made. Those who decide to follow Christ are no longer judged—they judge themselves, and thus enter a world made translucent in Christ, a transformed universe.

Seen in this perspective, the judgment is also the work of a redeeming love which must cut and burn before it can become eternal light. Our blindness, our darkness and our rebelliousness, indeed our whole inner being must be burnt, consumed and destroyed by the fire of Christ's love. The ruins of our own being will be cleared away and the site will be empty and ready to receive the new city, the eternal Jerusalem, which will come down out of heaven. We shall then begin to understand the mysterious saying in the vision which introduces the Revelation of John: 'When I saw him, I fell at his feet as though dead'.

John's account of his vision does not, however, end with those words. He goes on: 'But he laid his right hand upon me, saying, "Fear not, I am the first and the last, and the living one; I died, and behold I am alive for evermore, and I have the keys of death and Hades"' (Rev. 1 : 17–18).

The terrified disciple feels the tender pressure of Christ's right hand on him, the hand holding the seven stars. Jesus, victorious over death, has revealed a new world to all who believe in him—the world of eternal life. A Christian who has experienced the terror of encounter with Christ is always able to accept eternal life in the blinding glory of God's revelation. Jesus must and will lead us through that terrible experience of fear and threat. Then we shall be able to endure the intense joy that shatters our whole being and takes us eternally to God.

John can describe what takes place in this experience only by using all the precious imagery he can find; and yet, in the end, the experience of our eternity is indescribable. What awaits us and is indeed at hand is a state of eternal newness, a blessed transformation which changes us and fashions us so that we become more and more divine. In the words of the evangelist, 'I saw a new heaven and a new earth . . . I saw the holy city, new Jerusalem, coming down out of heaven from God, prepared as a bride adorned for her husband; and I heard a great voice from the throne saying: "Behold, the dwelling of God is with men. He will dwell with them, and they will be his people, and God himself will be with them. He will wipe away every tear from their eyes, and death shall be no more, neither shall there be mourning nor crying nor pain any more" . . . And he who sat on the throne said, "Behold, I make all things new . . . I am the Alpha and the Omega, the beginning and the end . . . He who conquers shall have this heritage, and I will be his God and he shall be my son" ' (Rev. 21 : 1–7).

Jesus' tender friendliness towards all men is revealed to us in the synoptic gospels and it is present equally in the teaching of John. At the same time, the power that breaks out of his writing is quite terrifying. We should willingly let this power take hold of us and carry us along towards the light and towards life. We should continue to live with Jesus and with the great demands that he makes. At the same time, we should always bear in mind that Christ is the light towards which we are moving, that he is life itself. Wherever we find life and wherever we are conscious of light, we are confronted, perhaps in a veiled form, but nonetheless really, by Christ himself.

We are called on to show a boundless concern for every creature and a tender awareness of every living being. Our Christian attitude will be marked by a profound respect for every honest viewpoint expressed by our fellow men and by an openness towards every aspect of the truth, wherever it may come from. It is from all this that heaven will be fashioned.

What we have to resist, however, above all in ourselves, is lies. A man or woman who lies and whose life is a lie is no friend of Christ's. Nothing can come from him except destruction. He falsifies man's being and prevents it from growing and developing. Life lived tenderly and unconditionally—that is the only true attitude for the one who imitates Christ. We know from John's image of Christ that we can only be Christians by being intolerant of sin wherever we find it, but at the same time boundlessly tolerant of sinners. That is John's prayer in the world.

The cosmic Christ

The cosmic Christ

The third and deepest level at which Christ is experienced is revealed in Paul's letters—especially in those to the Colossians and the Ephesians. These two letters were probably written when Paul was in prison in Rome awaiting trial. Isolated in his captivity, in a state of deep anxiety and oppressed on all sides, Paul was nonetheless able to interpret the universe in the light of his experience of Christ.

Paul's encounter with the Lord on the road to Damascus is at the centre of his experience of Christ, who appeared to him at that time as a blinding light. His experience was therefore very similar to John's—that of the risen Lord who had become entirely power and glory and for whom the limitations of time and space no longer existed. This Christ's words to Paul were mysterious: 'I am Jesus, whom you are persecuting'. The future apostle, however, had not persecuted Christ, but Christians. What must therefore have become quite clear to him when he heard these words was that there is no difference between Christ and those who believe in him: A Christian can become Christ; he can become one in his being with him.

What comes about between an individual Christian and Christ himself, in other words, is a 'relationship in existence'. Christ exists in the believer and the believer exists in Christ. This relationship is not simply a symbolic one—it is real and it includes all aspects of man's being. The existence of the one who believes in Christ is not something that stands alone. It is built up from Christ himself. That is the real mystery of the resurrection—Christ is able to fill a Christian's existence with his own bodily being, without in any way affecting a believer's personal unity. The Christian lives in Christ and Christ lives in him. We bear Christ in us and Christ bears us in himself. This relationship in existence therefore unites individual Christians to each other in a single community. The risen Christ bears all Christians bodily in himself and brings them together into one being. Because he has been raised up above the state of restriction to time and space here on earth, he is able to reach men of all times and places and make them bodily members of his own risen body. He can accept them into himself and open himself to them so that they are changed by him. This growing together with Christ brings about a real unity between all Christians, although the personal individuality of each Christian does not cease to exist.

We build Christ up. Throughout the whole of history, Christ's birth is always taking place. One of the most profound insights of the apostle Paul is that, although Christ has already come, he nonetheless continues to become until the end of the world. At the end of time is the 'fulness of Christ'—the 'full Christ'.

The sacramental sign of this embodiment in Christ—Christ's birth throughout the history of man—is baptism. In baptism, we receive the life of Christ, but only, as it were, as a dynamic tendency, a power which will fashion us into Christ and bring us, in time, to the fulness of his life. Impelled forward by the dynamic power of grace, a

Christian can grow more deeply into unity with the risen Christ, enter more closely into community with him, and let himself be fashioned more perfectly according to Christ's image.

In Paul's view, then, baptism is really the whole of Christian life—a growth into the being of the risen Christ. In this process, a Christian becomes more and more profoundly conscious of his growing union with Christ and of his own resurrection. With all baptized Christians, he builds up the Christ who will appear again at the end of time. He plunges into Christ's being with his own existence as a Christian and is again and again made new until the last act of his baptism is accomplished. This final act is his own death, when he at last becomes entirely one in the reality of the risen Christ.

Ultimately, however, this relationship in existence goes beyond the sphere of man's life and embraces the whole world. The power of the risen Christ extends to the universe itself. Everything in heaven and on earth is included and summed up in Christ. The whole universe was filled to overflowing and fulfilled when Christ rose again from the dead and ascended into heaven. In every part of the world, Christ is present as the mysterious quintessence of all creation.

For us who believe in him the universe is the translucent reality of Christ himself. We can always discover him as the God-man at the heart of all things. Communion with the world is communion with the inner truth of the visible reality of Jesus Christ. This fundamental idea of Paul's was expressed thus by Ambrose, the fourth-century Bishop of Milan: 'In him the earth has risen again; in him heaven has risen; in him the world has risen'. In his treatise on the first beginnings, Origen said: 'Jesus is everywhere. He permeates the whole universe'. Paschasius Radbertus wrote in his ninth-century commentary on the gospel according to Matthew: 'We should never confine our search for Christ, who fills all things, to any one restricted place'.

In this context Karl Rahner emphasizes the idea of community: 'What we call the resurrection of Christ and regard as his private destiny is only . . . the first symptom of the total change that has already begun to take place behind the experience in the true and really decisive depth of all things. Christ's resurrection is the first eruption of a volcano, since it shows that the interior of the world is already burning with God's fire, which will eventually make everything glow . . . Christ is already in the midst of all the poor things of this earth. Our world is no longer an abyss between God and man . . . Christ is present in it and he is the heart of our world and the mysterious seal set on it, making it eternally valid. We, as believers, are bound to love this earth because God dwells in it . . . In the resurrection of Christ, God has shown us his acceptance of our world for ever.'

Heaven will be the final revelation of what is taking place here and now in a mysterious and hidden manner. That is the ultimate disclosure of the growing of mankind and the world into union with each other and with Christ. Until that is finally accomplished in his death, each Christian must penetrate more and more deeply into the risen Christ, becoming more and more tranquil, patient, understanding, self-sacrificing, humble and kind. In these mature Christian acts, we already bring about our own resurrection and ascension. Heaven rises up out of all these hidden activities. This heaven is Christ himself built up from our being as men and enveloped in a glorified world. Teilhard de Chardin, who was deeply influenced by Paul's thought, called this 'Christ clothed in the world'. By our imitation of Christ, we are able to give the earth nothing less than heaven—the risen Christ. In this way, with our co-operation, Christ becomes the mediator of a cosmic and universal resurrection and ascension. That is the ultimate and deepest mystery of Christian life.

The end of time

The end of time

To conclude these meditations, I should like to discuss some modern ideas which may help Christians to answer the questions they are asked about the end of time.

The end is the real beginning

The most important message of the New Covenant is that an entirely new dimension of being has been revealed in Jesus, to which the name 'heaven' has been given. This heaven grows in the children of God, who are the brothers and sisters of Jesus. A Christian can't think of man simply in the light of his presence on earth. His life is so conceived that it points towards heaven; towards a state which is very near but, either in spite or because of this, isn't here yet.

Most of the life of any individual and of mankind as a whole has always, throughout history, consisted of painful, tentative seeking. All the searching that has so far taken place is no more than the first birth pangs. The world will only really come into being when man enters heaven. In the deepest sense of the word, we are not yet alive. We are not yet really able to see, hear or understand the total reality. Life is not yet present—it is simply coming forward to meet us. Man's being and the world are still, as it were, in the front line.

The world is moving towards fulfilment

The world is still being born. Everything is developing
from an original state of being—developing towards life.
Life is moving towards fulfilment in the process of man's
transformation into spirit. The spirit succeeds in understanding itself by knowing God and responding to him
in total love. As men become more fully united with God
and each other, the world moves more surely in the
direction of ultimate fulfilment. That fulfilment is a state
which is eternally translucent to God.

The universe is a single unity which is not yet.
Creation itself is still in a state of becoming. God creates
the world by giving it the power to evolve over millions
of years, but always in an upward direction, towards him.
But the history of the evolution of the world and of man's
growth is always a history of salvation. It is the birth of
what is eternally valid from the womb of the earth. In
our cosmos, there is no profane sphere of becoming.

Creation is christological

'For us men and for our salvation he came down from
heaven.' That is the answer of the creed to the age-old
question 'Why did God become man?'

Two reasons are given. The first is that he became man
'for us men'; in other words, so that man can become
himself, so that he can really be man. The second reason
is 'for our salvation'; in other words, so that he could
redeem us from our guilt. Those are the two basic func-
tions of Christ in the history of man's salvation.

Christ raises man's being—and with it the universe,
which is concentrated in us—to fulfilment. He is the
ultimately created man, the summit towards which the

world is moving. He draws everything towards himself: forwards and upward into the sphere of glorification. In this sense, Christ is the God who raises up. In his letter to the Colossians, Paul says of this cosmic Christ: 'In him all things were created, in heaven and on earth . . . All things were created through him and for him. He is before all things, and in him all things hold together' (Col. 1:16–17).

From the beginning and at all times, the cosmos is moving towards Christ. Christ is the 'predestined world' and, in the course of millions of years, the movement of being is narrowed down and concentrated on one point of reference, which is Omega point, the Logos who has become man. The evolution of the world preceding his appearance is a preparation for the emergence of man. This total evolution, which converges in the historical figure of Christ, then moves beyond the whole spectrum of the cosmos and of human history and embraces the total reality.

On the one hand, the universe acquires life in being directed towards Christ and finds its fulfilment as man. (This is the incarnation of the world.) Man, on the other hand, becomes increasingly conscious and capable of decision. The further he advances in this direction, the more decisively he is confronted with God. (This is the incarnation of man.) Finally, in becoming man, God combines all the power of the world and of mankind within himself and takes it in his great exodus—his death, resurrection and ascension into heaven—to its ultimate fulfilment. (This is the incarnation of God.)

That is the basic structure of the creation; of the creative process of a world so conceived that it is directed towards Christ.

Unending progress

Our ultimate fulfilment—heaven—will be found in our sharing, as creatures, in God's being. No creature can, however, entirely absorb or exhaust the infinite fulness of God. Our being can never become completely identified with God's infinite being. Even in heaven, all fulfilment is also a new beginning, the commencement of a further search and of even greater fulfilment. Heaven is therefore essentially an endless dynamic power. Fulfilment itself will so 'extend' our souls that we shall be able to be even more filled and fulfilled by God's being immediately afterwards.

We are therefore, in this sense, eternally seeking God, who will always be greater than our finite being. God who is ultimately found is not God. We seek God in order to find him, during our life on earth. After having found him, we go on seeking him in eternal blessedness. He remains concealed, however, so that we shall look for him in order to find him. He remains immeasurable, so that we shall go on looking for him after having found him.

In this way, our eternity is an endless progress, a continuous movement into God. All that is static here becomes, in the eternity of heaven, infinitely dynamic. Nothing can become motionless and rigid in heaven. Fulfilment is eternal change, a state of endless, uninterrupted life.

If we meditate about this and allow it to penetrate effectively into our Christian consciousness, we shall eventually come to recognize that . . .

A message of joy

. . . Our destiny and that of the world we inhabit was decided when Christ rose from the dead. Whether we live consciously or unconsciously as Christians (that is, in Christ), we are all going forward in the direction of heaven. Our ultimate end is always already working in everything in the world that is apparently transitional. No search ever ends in a vacuum.

Nothing, Paul said in his letter to the Romans, will ever be able to separate us from the love of Christ (Rom. 8 : 35ff). Nothing—except a rejection of Christ's love. We have already attained freedom, openness and joy. The Christ of the Apocalypse declared : 'I have set before you an open door, which no one is able to shut' (Rev. 3 : 8). Wherever a small flame of genuine love burns, there is the light of heaven, already visibly present. No hope is ever in vain. We lose nothing. Ultimately, we cannot lose anything that we go without in our lives on earth. We have no reason to be despondent or despairing. The whole of Christianity can, seen in this perspective, be summarized as the faith in which God says Yes to our longings, and goes so far beyond them that even our most audacious hopes and dreams sometimes seem faint-hearted and lacking in faith.

What, then, is the basic attitude of a Christian who wishes to understand the ultimate reality? He should approach it positively, with openness and joy. Gloom has no place here. It is negative and valueless and it will lead him past the mystery of the end of time, not into it. That positive attitude should also characterize his intellectual struggle with the questions raised by the doctrine of the 'last things'. He will then recognize and learn to express the fundamental realities of the end of time.

What are those realities? They are that life is always a process of becoming. The whole universe is included in

God's salvation. In the end the cosmos is fulfilled in Christ. That fulfilment is a process of constant transformation, making us and our world more and more divine. What God has prepared for us is, quite simply, infinite joy.